CLASSICAL THEMES FOR TWO

Arrangements by Peter Deneff

ISBN 978-1-5400-1413-9

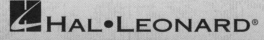

7777 W. BLUEMOUND RD. P.O. BOX 13819 MILWAUKEE, WI 53213

In Australia Contact:
Hal Leonard Australia Pty. Ltd.
4 Lentara Court
Cheltenham, Victoria, 3192 Australia
Email: ausadmin@halleonard.com.au

Visit Hal Leonard Online at
www.halleonard.com

ACADEMIC FESTIVAL OVERTURE

ALTO SAXES

By JOHANNES BRAHMS

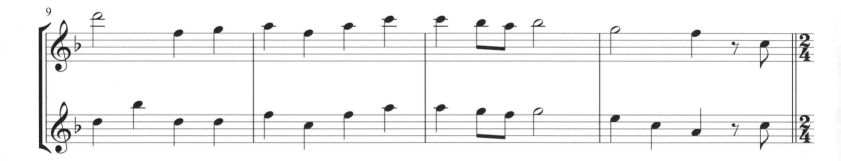

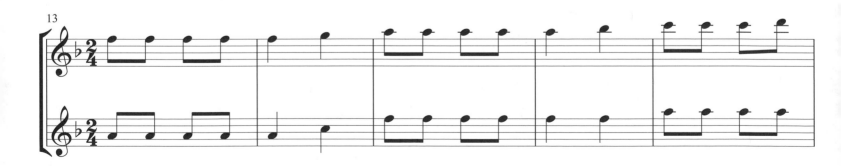

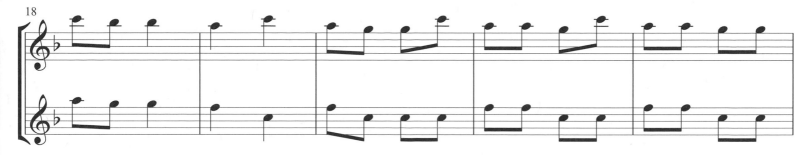

AIR
from WATER MUSIC

ALTO SAXES

By GEORGE FRIDERIC HANDEL

Andante con moto

(small notes optional)

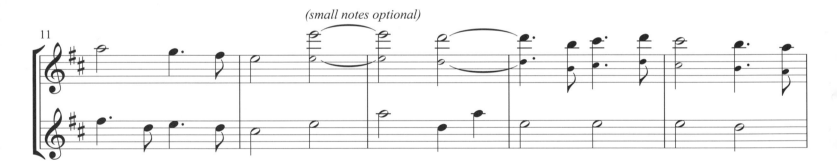

To Coda ⊕

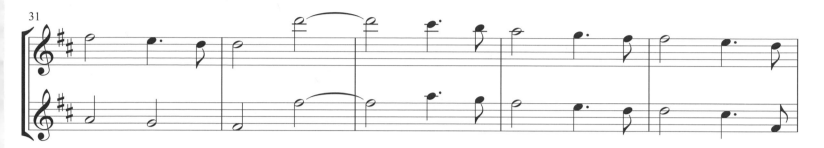

D.C. al Coda

CODA

AIR ON THE G STRING
from ORCHESTRAL SUITE NO. 3 IN D MAJOR, BWV 1068

ALTO SAXES

By JOHANN SEBASTIAN BACH

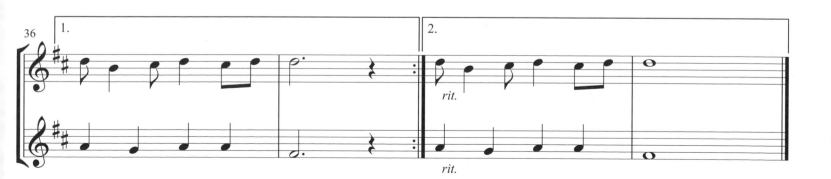

BLUE DANUBE WALTZ

ALTO SAXES

By JOHANN STRAUSS, JR.

Moderately

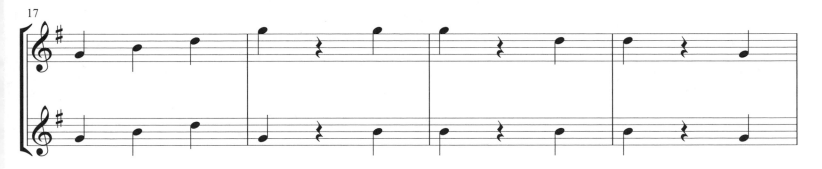

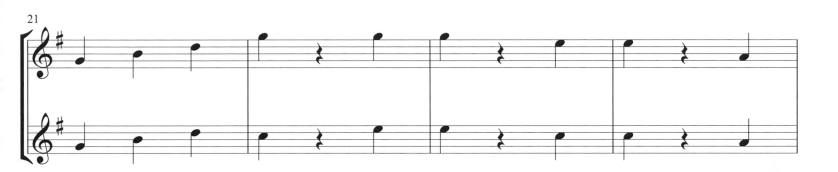

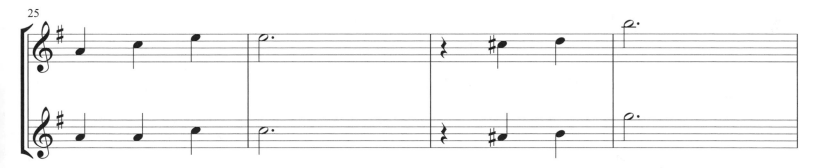

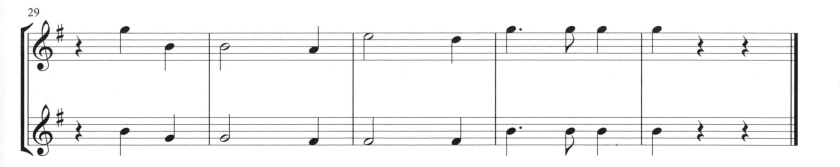

CANON IN D

ALTO SAXES

By JOHANN PACHELBEL

Moderately

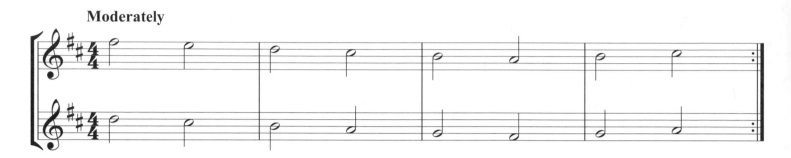

CLAIR DE LUNE
from SUITE BERGAMASQUE

ALTO SAXES

By CLAUDE DEBUSSY

Andante

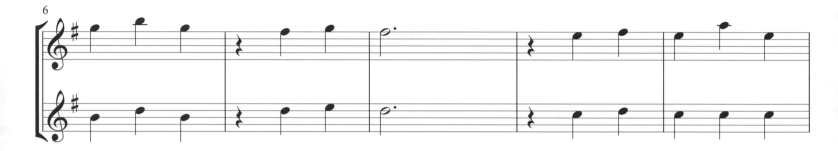

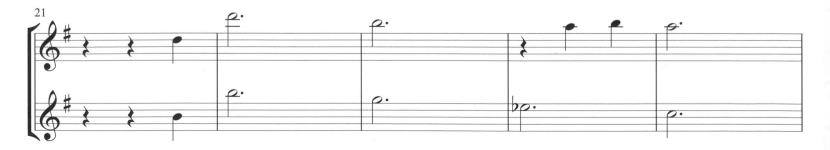

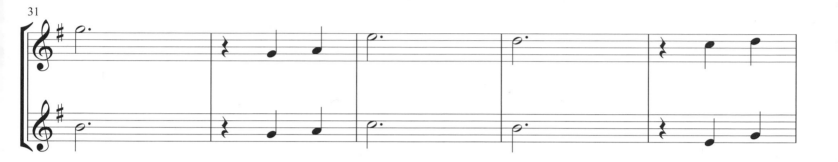

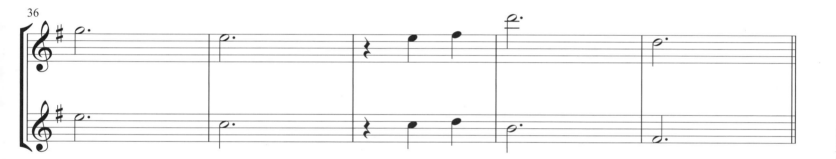

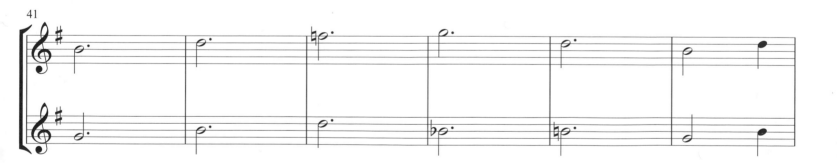

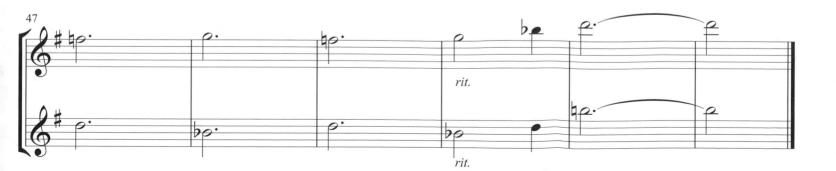

EINE KLEINE NACHTMUSIK
(Second Movement Theme: "Romance")

ALTO SAXES

By WOLFGANG AMADEUS MOZART

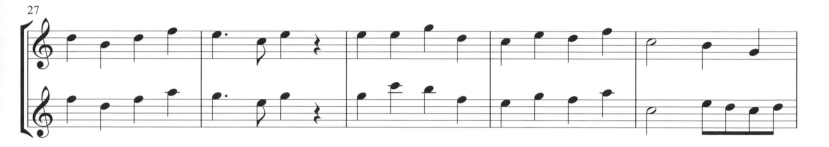

FLOWER DUET
from LAKMÉ

ALTO SAXES

By LÉO DELIBES

Andante con moto

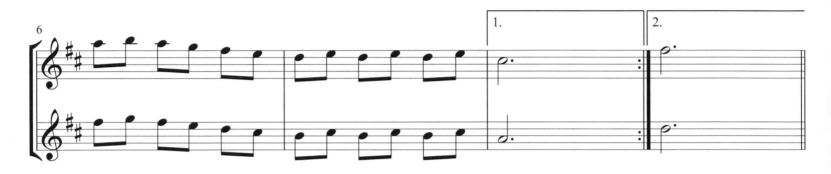

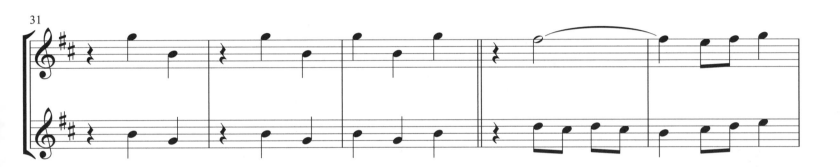

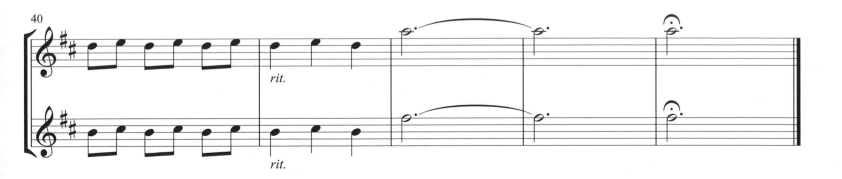

HALLELUJAH CHORUS
from MESSIAH

ALTO SAXES

By GEORGE FRIDERIC HANDEL

Allegro

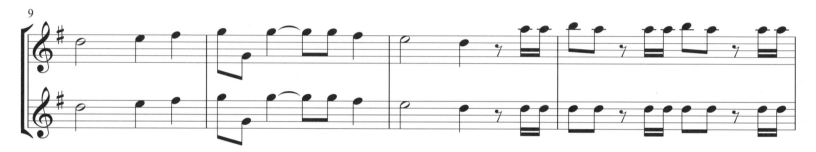

(small note optional)

HORNPIPE
from WATER MUSIC

ALTO SAXES

By GEORGE FRIDERIC HANDEL

Allegro maestoso

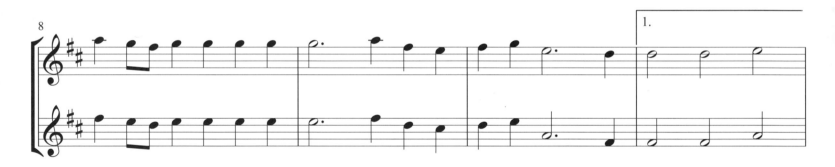

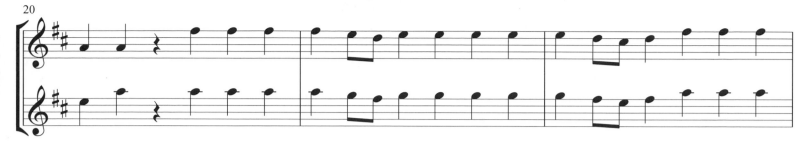

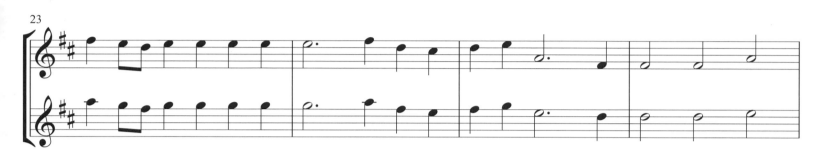

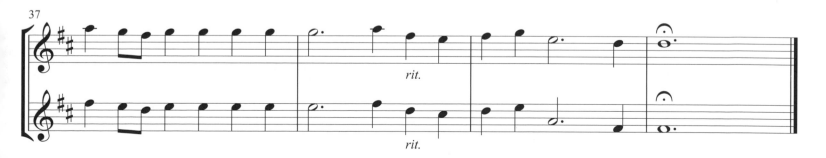

HUNGARIAN DANCE NO. 5

ALTO SAXES

By JOHANNES BRAHMS

To Coda ⊕

1.

2.

D.C. al Coda

CODA
⊕

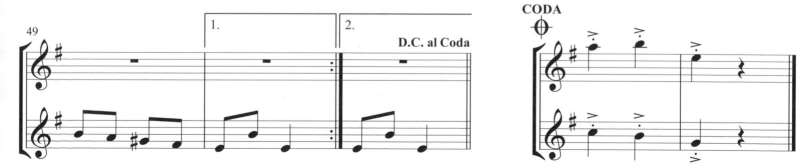

JESU, JOY OF MAN'S DESIRING

from CANTATA 147

ALTO SAXES

By JOHANN SEBASTIAN BACH

D.C. al Coda

CODA

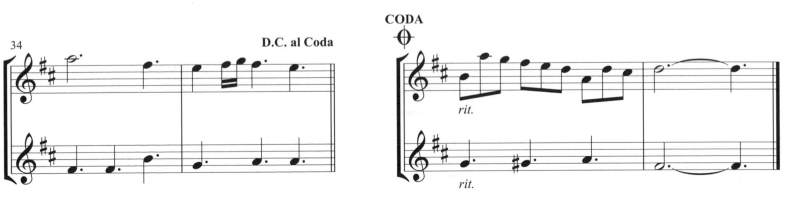

rit.

rit.

MARCH
from THE NUTCRACKER

ALTO SAXES

By PYOTR IL'YICH TCHAIKOVSKY

March tempo

MINUET IN G
from ANNA MAGDALENA NOTEBOOK

ALTO SAXES

By CHRISTIAN PETZOLD
formerly attributed to J.S. Bach

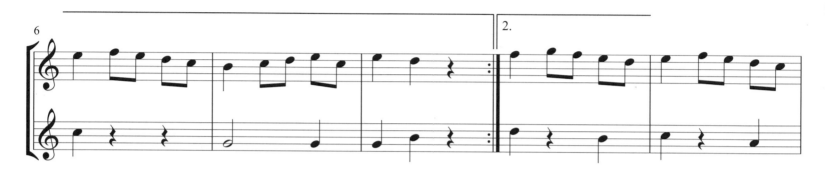

ODE TO JOY
from SYMPHONY NO. 9 IN D MINOR

ALTO SAXES

By LUDWIG VAN BEETHOVEN

Allegro

MORNING
from PEER GYNT

ALTO SAXES

By EDVARD GRIEG

Allegretto pastorale

PICTURES AT AN EXHIBITION
(Promenade)

ALTO SAXES

By MODEST MUSSORGSKY

POMP AND CIRCUMSTANCE
March No. 1

ALTO SAXES

By EDWARD ELGAR

Allegro

RONDEAU
from SUITE DE SYMPHONIE

ALTO SAXES

By JEAN-JOSEPH MOURET

Moderately

SHEEP MAY SAFELY GRAZE

from CANTATA 208

ALTO SAXES

By JOHANN SEBASTIAN BACH

THE SURPRISE SYMPHONY
(Symphony No. 94, Second Movement Theme)

ALTO SAXES

By FRANZ JOSEPH HAYDN

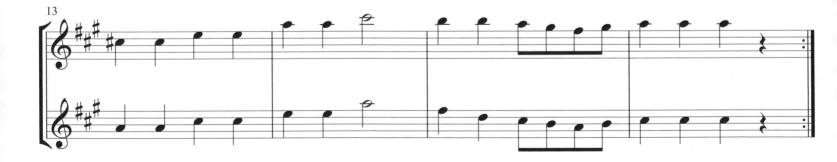

SYMPHONY NO. 7
(Second Movement Theme)

ALTO SAXES

By LUDWIG VAN BEETHOVEN

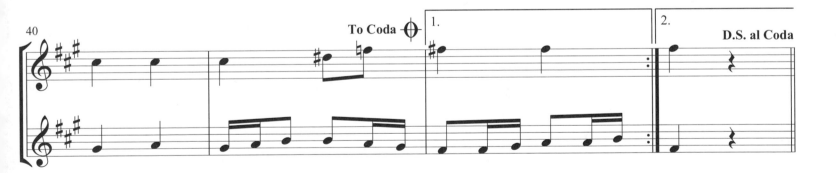

TRUMPET VOLUNTARY
(Prince of Denmark's March)

ALTO SAXES

By JEREMIAH CLARKE

Moderately

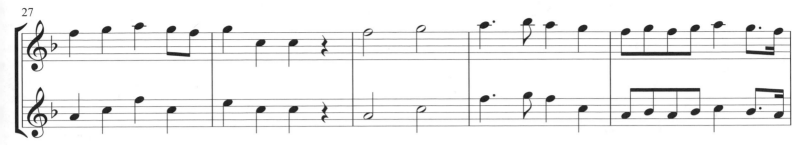

WILLIAM TELL OVERTURE
(Theme)

ALTO SAXES

By GIOACHINO ROSSINI